The Application of
the Interpretation
of the New Jerusalem
to the Seeking Believers

Witness Lee

Living Stream Ministry
Anaheim, California • www.lsm.org

First Edition, December 1995.

ISBN 978-0-87083-959-7

Published by

Living Stream Ministry
2431 W. La Palma Ave., Anaheim, CA 92801 U.S.A.
P. O. Box 2121, Anaheim, CA 92814 U.S.A.

Printed and bound by CPI Group (UK) Ltd, Croydon, CR0 4YY

08   09   10   11   12   13   /   13   12   11   10   9   8   7

CONTENTS

PREFACE

This book is composed of messages given by Brother Witness Lee in Anaheim, California on November 23-25, 1995.

THE APPLICATION OF THE INTERPRETATION OF THE NEW JERUSALEM TO THE SEEKING BELIEVERS

MESSAGE ONE

ITS SIGNIFICANCE AND ITS BASE

Scripture Reading: Rev. 21:2-3, 9-10, 18b, 21b-22; 22:1-2

OUTLINE

I. Its significance:
  A. The New Jerusalem is the greatest and the ultimate sign in the Scriptures—Rev. 21:2, 9-10.
  B. It signifies an organic constitution of the processed Triune God mingled with His regenerated, transformed, and glorified tripartite elect:
    1. According to its humanity, it is the tabernacle of God among men—the dwelling place of God in His humanity among men on the earth—21:3.
    2. According to its divinity, it is the temple of God as the dwelling place of His redeemed elect—21:22.
    3. According to its humanity, it is the human wife (with the divine life and nature) of the Lamb—the redeeming God—21:2, 9.
    4. According to its divinity, it is the divine Husband (the redeeming God in His consummated embodiment, Christ, with the human life and nature) of God's redeemed elect.

II. Its base:
  A. It is pure gold, signifying the divine nature of God as the base for its building—21:18b.
  B. It is the solid foundation of its throne for the divine administration—22:1b:

1. Proceeding from this administration the river of the water of life, signifying the Spirit, in the middle of its street as the supply to the entire city—22:1a.
2. In the river growing the tree of life, signifying Christ, as the main supply to the entire city through the river—22:2.
3. Proceeding from this glorious center the divine and human communication, signified by the street, to reach all twelve gates of the city, in order to bring the entire city into the submission to the one divine administration and to blend the entire city into the oneness of the one divinity-mingled-with-humanity communication (fellowship)—21:21b.

Prayer: Lord, we thank You that we could have this conference with thousands of seekers coming here to seek after You according to Your revelation and vision. Lord, open up this mysterious book to all of us. Grant us, Lord, the understanding. Grant us also the inner seeing. Lord, we trust in You. Sustain us and maintain us to the end. Amen.

The subject of these messages is the application of the interpretation of the New Jerusalem to the seeking believers. The burden for the messages in this book can be expressed in the following four statements:

1. The New Jerusalem is the greatest and the ultimate sign in the Scriptures, signifying an organic constitution of the processed Triune God mingled with His regenerated, transformed, and glorified tripartite elect.

2. Its base is pure gold, signifying the divine nature of God; it is the solid foundation of its throne for the divine administration, which is the glorious center from which proceeds the divine and human communication, signified by its street, to reach all its twelve gates.

3. Its gates are pearls, signifying the issue of the secretion of Christ's redeeming and life-releasing death and His life-dispensing resurrection.

4. Its wall and its foundations are precious stones, consummated by the Spirit through His transforming and building work.

In the past we released many messages to interpret this section of the Word on the mystery of the New Jerusalem. Thus, there is no need for us to repeat any past interpretation. We want to go on to apply to ourselves what has already been interpreted. In this first message, we want to see and enter into the application of the significance and the base of the New Jerusalem.

I. ITS SIGNIFICANCE

A. The New Jerusalem Being the Greatest and the Ultimate Sign in the Scriptures

Revelation 1:1 says that the Lord Jesus sent His angel to John to make His revelation known by signs, so the New

Jerusalem is the greatest and the ultimate sign in the Scriptures (21:2, 9-10). A sign is a symbol with spiritual significance.

B. Signifying an Organic Constitution
of the Processed Triune God
Mingled with His Regenerated, Transformed,
and Glorified Tripartite Elect

The New Jerusalem is a city, but this city is not literally physical. It is a sign, a figure, signifying an organic constitution. It is not something organized, but something constituted organically. The holy city is a constitution in life of the processed Triune God mingled with His regenerated, transformed, and glorified tripartite elect. It is an organic constitution of two parties: God and man. The first party is divine. The second party is human.

1. The Tabernacle of God

The New Jerusalem has two natures, humanity and divinity. According to its humanity, the New Jerusalem is the tabernacle of God among men— the dwelling place of God in His humanity among men on the earth (Rev. 21:3). In the Bible, the tabernacle is a human dwelling place. The New Jerusalem is a human dwelling place because it is constituted with humanity. It is God's human dwelling place on earth. John 1:14 says that God was incarnated in the flesh to tabernacle among men. He is God, but He has become a man. He partook of humanity as His nature, so He dwells in humanity.

2. The Temple of God

According to its divinity, the New Jerusalem is the temple of God as the dwelling place of His redeemed elect (Rev. 21:22). The holy city is the temple of God because it is divine. It is the temple of God, yet it is the dwelling place of His redeemed. How could this be? Because this is God's temple, the dweller must be divine, but what about us? Are we divine or human? According to its humanity, the New Jerusalem is the tabernacle, but God dwells in the tabernacle. God can dwell in a human dwelling place because He has become a man. According to the divinity of the New Jerusalem, it is a temple for God to dwell in. If you are only human and not divine, you cannot dwell in the temple. We human beings can dwell in a divine temple because we have been made God in life and in nature but not in the Godhead. The New Jerusalem is a mutual abode. According to its humanity, it is a human tabernacle. According to its divinity, it is a divine temple. It is a human dwelling place, but the Dweller is God. How can God dwell in a human place? Because He became a man. In the same way, how can we humans dwell in God's temple? Because we have been made God. This is the mutual abiding of God and man.

3. The Human Wife of the Redeeming God

According to its humanity, the New Jerusalem is the human wife (with the divine life and nature) of the Lamb— the redeeming God (21:2, 9). This human wife can marry a divine Person because she has the divine life and nature. This qualifies her to match the redeeming God. On the one hand, she is human. On the other hand, she is divine. Because she is human, she can be the redeeming God's human wife. Because she is divine, she can marry Him, a divine Person.

4. The Divine Husband of God's Redeemed Elect

According to its divinity, it is the divine Husband (the redeeming God in His consummated embodiment, Christ, with the human life and nature) of God's redeemed elect. The wife is human, and the Husband is divine. How can a human wife marry a divine Person? Because she has the divine Person's divine nature and life. How can the same entity also be a husband? Because the New Jerusalem is divine. The divine God is a part of its constituent. Therefore, on the one hand, it is a wife. On the other hand, it is a husband. The New Jerusalem is the wife according to its humanity and the husband according to its divinity. But as the divine Husband, the New Jerusalem has the human life and nature. In its humanity and in its divinity it is both a mutual abode and a couple, a wife and a husband.

II. ITS BASE

A. Pure Gold

The base of the New Jerusalem is pure gold, signifying the divine nature of God as the base for its building (21:18b). The New Jerusalem is a golden mountain. Because we are the constituents of this New Jerusalem, we must be gold. We were made of dust, but when we received Christ as our life, we were regenerated into gold. In regeneration we received the divine life, the golden life. In the old creation, represented by Adam, we were dusty men, but when we were regenerated, we became golden men.

B. The Solid Foundation of Its Throne for the Divine Administration

The base of the New Jerusalem is the solid foundation of the divine throne for the divine administration (22:1b). The river of water of life, signifying the Spirit, proceeds from this administration in the middle of the New Jerusalem's street as the supply to the entire city (v. 1a). In the river grows the tree of life, signifying Christ, as the main supply to the entire city through the river (v. 2). The divine and human communication, signified by the street, proceeds from this glorious center to reach all twelve gates of the city, in order to bring the entire city into the submission to the one divine administration and to blend the entire city into the oneness of the one divinity-mingled-with-humanity communication, fellowship (21:21b).

The throne on which God reigns is the center of the glory of the New Jerusalem. It signifies God's ruling, God's reigning. A street comes out from the throne. This street connected to the throne is for communication and mainly for the throne's administration. The divine ruling has the divine administration.

On the street there is the traffic, the going and coming. First, the street is for God's going and coming, which are for God's administration. Eventually, this street becomes a "fellowship street." This fellowship is between the redeeming God and His redeemed people. The redeeming God and His redeemed people must have going and coming fellowship. Not only so, God's redeemed people must have going and coming fellowship among themselves.

From the throne proceeds the river of water of life, signifying the Spirit, and this Spirit is God's flowing out. On the throne, God is the Ruler. He is the One who reigns. But when He comes out, He is the Spirit. In the middle of the street is the river, which is God proceeding out to be life as water to quench the thirst of the entire city. First, the city has a throne and second, a street for administration and fellowship. Third, in the fellowship is the river of water of life. Fourth, there is the tree of life, signifying the second Person of the Godhead.

God flows out in the third Person of the Trinity. Then the second Person of the Trinity is Christ, the Son of God, as the tree of life that grows in the river and along its two sides to supply life to nourish the entire city. This picture shows us that with the fellowship street we enjoy the Spirit as the river and Christ as the tree of life. These three things—the street, the river, and the tree of life—reach all the twelve gates, which signify God's redeemed elect. The divine fellowship brings God to all His redeemed people, to all the twelve gates, to bring all His redeemed people back to Himself. First, the street goes from the throne to the twelve gates. Then it comes from the twelve gates to the throne.

Now let us consider the application of this fellowship. In applying this I would like to ask, "Before you were saved, who was your ruler? What was your administration?" You yourself tried to be your own ruler and you were a mess. Actually, you had no ruler or administration. One day you heard the gospel, which said, "Repent, for the kingdom of the heavens has drawn near" (Matt. 3:2). You needed to repent to come under the ruling of God's kingdom. Before that time you were a person with no ruler and no administration. But you repented to the divine Ruler and came under His administration. Through the gospel God came to be your kingdom. He is the King on the throne. Connected to His throne is a street on which you should walk, and that street is His administration. From the day you repented, you have felt that there is a throne and a golden street, a golden administration, within you. Then you began to do things according to the gold, according to the nature of God. This is because both the throne and the street are built on the gold as the nature of God.

When the brothers are buying a tie, they should buy it according to the divine nature within them. Today the shallow gospel never touches this matter. But in the high peak of the gospel we have to see this. The gospel brings us back to God as our throne, to God as our administration. We have to live a life in which we do everything according to God's nature. Ephesians 4 says that we should let no corrupt word proceed out of our mouth (v. 29). This is because we are children of God. When we speak anything, we need to remember that we are God's children; we are golden. To speak corrupt things does not match our golden nature. Our nature today is no longer just dusty but golden. If we take this word, it will change our life. We will be adjusted and regulated by the golden nature of God in all that we do. The sisters would not spend so much time to style their hair. That is not according to the golden throne, the golden administration.

All of our fellowship should be according to God's golden nature. The river is in the middle of the street, and the street is the golden nature. In this fellowship is the river, the Holy Spirit, as our beverage and our supply to quench our thirst. Then we also have Christ as the tree of life for our life supply to nourish us. In order to experience all of this, we must be on the golden street, the base of gold. We may feel that it is enough to say that our fellowship with God is our contacting God, and our fellowship with the saints is our contacting the saints. But this is not the deciding factor concerning whether or not our fellowship is the fellowship of God. The fellowship of God must be based upon God's divine nature. I may go to visit a certain brother every day, but is that the real fellowship? Whether that is the real fellowship or not is determined by whether or not it is based upon the golden nature within me. If my contact with a brother is not based upon the golden nature, then I am making a natural friendship with him. I am not practicing the spiritual fellowship of life based upon God's divine nature.

As we enter into the experience and application of the divine nature of God, we make ourselves genuine parts of the New Jerusalem. Eventually, we become golden in everything. Every department store is a place of temptation where we can depart from the golden nature to buy things. Even in the church life, we can make natural friendships with certain saints, but that is not the genuine fellowship. Fellowship should be based upon the golden nature within us. If we practice this fellowship, we are living as a part of the New Jerusalem. We become the constituents of the New Jerusalem. This is not according to our outward doing but according to our inward being. The inward being of our Christian life must be God's golden nature. We should live, walk, and do everything based upon the golden nature within us.

This is the application of the interpretation of the golden base of the New Jerusalem to the seeking believers. Because God has released the high peak of the divine revelation to us, we all have to learn the high and new language to speak forth the revelation of the New Jerusalem as the greatest and ultimate sign in the Scriptures.

THE APPLICATION OF THE INTERPRETATION OF THE NEW JERUSALEM TO THE SEEKING BELIEVERS

MESSAGE TWO

ITS GATES

Scripture Reading: Rev. 21:12b-13, 21a

OUTLINE

I. Its gates are pearls—Rev. 21:21a:
   A. Signifying the issue of the secretion of Christ's redeeming and life-releasing death and His life-dispensing resurrection.
   B. Both kinds of secretion (dispensing) require the seeking believers' daily experience of the death of Christ subjectively by the power of Christ's resurrection that they may be conformed to the death of Christ (Phil. 3:10), and their daily experience of the resurrection of Christ subjectively by the bountiful supply of the Spirit (the reality of resurrection) of Jesus Christ that they may be conformed to the image of the firstborn Son of God (Phil. 1:19; Rom. 8:29).

II. Its entry—Rev. 21:12b-13:
   A. Such an entry into the New Jerusalem to partake of the tree of life has been established by Christ through His death and resurrection, fulfilling the righteous requirements of God according to the law of Israel in the Old Testament so that the closed way to the tree of life is reopened to the seeking believers.
   B. This reopened way to partake of the tree of life by entering into the New Jerusalem is universally available to the four directions of the earth with

three gates on each of the four sides of the holy city, signifying that the processed and consummated Triune God is willingly open to receive the repentant sinners into the ultimate consummation of His eternal economy.

Prayer: Lord, we thank You for this meeting. We ask You to do a particular thing—to show us the second application of the New Jerusalem. Thank You for the last message. You have shown us the first application. Amen.

In the previous message, the Lord has shown us the first application of the New Jerusalem. To apply the base of the New Jerusalem, we must have our being and do everything in our walk and work for the Lord to participate in His move based upon the golden nature of God. The building up of the New Jerusalem, which is a golden mount, is to make us divine, golden. The sisters' fellowship must be based upon the golden nature of God. We co-workers who are participating in the Lord's move bear a heavy burden. We have to realize that our move in the Lord's move should be based upon His golden nature. The first application of the New Jerusalem is to have everything that belongs to us based upon God's golden nature to make us golden, divine, day by day. When this is completed, that will be the consummation of the building up of the golden mount, the golden city.

I. ITS GATES BEING PEARLS

Now we come to the second application of the New Jerusalem, which is altogether related to the gates. Its gates are pearls (Rev. 21:21a). As we have seen, the entire New Jerusalem is a great sign. Its twelve gates are twelve big pearls. It is impossible for natural pearls to be so big that they can be the gates of the city. The pearl in the city is not a natural pearl but is used by God as a sign.

A. The Issue of a Twofold Secretion

When an oyster is wounded by a grain of sand, it secretes its life-juice around the grain of sand and makes it into a precious pearl. Pearls signify the issue of Christ's secretion in two aspects: His redeeming and life-releasing death and His life-dispensing resurrection. Without God's revelation we can never realize that the death of Christ secretes, dispenses, to produce the gates of the city. The twelve gates are the issue of Christ's secretion also in His life-dispensing resurrection. He resurrected to be the life-giving Spirit to dispense the divine life into the believers (1 Cor. 15:45b). This is a kind of secretion issuing in a big pearl to be the gates of the city. Both Christ's death and resurrection have an issue, a secretion.

B. Requiring the Seeking Believers' Daily Experience of the Death and Resurrection of Christ

Both kinds of secretion (dispensing) require the seeking believers' daily experience of the death of Christ subjectively by the power of Christ's resurrection that they may be conformed to the death of Christ (Phil. 3:10). We have to put not just Christ's death itself but the secretion of His death into our daily experience subjectively. We may know that we have been crucified with Christ, but we need to experience this. When a couple is quarreling, is that the talk of ones who are being crucified? When a brother talks to his wife, he has to consider that he is a crucified person.

Stanza 2 of hymn #938 (*Hymns*), a short song for baptism, says, "No longer I! No longer I! / Christ in me I'll testify!" In our baptism we declared that we were finished. It is no more I, but Christ who lives in me (Gal. 2:20). In our subjective experience, we should be on the cross. We may know this teaching, but in our daily experience we are short. In our daily life, we do not practice being crucified with Christ.

A number of times when I was irritated at my wife, I tried to argue with her. But when the word of my argument came to the tip of my tongue, I was reminded—"Is this being crucified on the cross?" Right away I stopped. I went to my study room and prayed, "Lord, forgive me. I know I have been crucified, but I don't practice it. What a shame, Lord! I have been following You for over sixty years, yet I would still try to argue with my dear wife. Still I live and not Christ. I have been teaching others about this for more than sixty years, but I did not apply what I taught."

Dear saints, the second application of the New Jerusalem is for us to experience subjectively the death of Christ in our daily life. We cannot do this in and by ourselves. None of us can practice such a thing. Everybody likes to argue. Argument comes from our natural life, from "I" not Christ. But we should have this "I" all the time crucified on the cross. We have to put this application of the subjective death of Christ into our daily experience. We can experience His death only by the power of the resurrection of Christ.

The chorus of hymn #631 says, "If no death, no life." This life comes to us not by our natural life but by the power of Christ's resurrection. Yes, we have been crucified, but how can we keep ourselves on the cross all the time? No human being can do it except those who know the power of the resurrection of Christ; they have the capacity, the ability, to practice this. By the power of the resurrection of Christ, we have the ability and the power to keep our pitiful self on the cross. How can a sister be a good wife? A good wife is a crucified wife, a wife on the cross.

We are required to remain on the cross under the crucifixion all the time. Sometimes I went to the Lord and said, "Lord, I cannot carry out this kind of Christian life. I thought that after I believed in You, You would do good things for me." The Lord answered, "Yes, I will do everything good for you, but you have to remain on the cross. As long as you live by yourself, I can do nothing for you. I can do something for you only if you remain on the cross." I said, "Lord, how can I do it? I have no power to do it." The Lord said, "I am in you, I am the resurrection, and I have the power to enable you to remain on the cross." Stanza 1 of hymn #631 says, "If I'd know Christ's risen power, / I must ever love the Cross." Life is Christ. If I am going to live Christ out, I have to remain on the cross to die there. This is the second application of the New Jerusalem. The New Jerusalem has twelve gates, and they should be applied to our daily life by our keeping ourselves crucified all the time in our daily experience that we could be conformed to Christ's death.

The believers also should seek the daily experience of the resurrection of Christ subjectively by the bountiful supply of the Spirit (the reality of resurrection) of Jesus Christ that they may be conformed to the image of the firstborn Son of God (Phil. 1:19; Rom. 8:29). We are required to do two things: to experience Christ's death subjectively in our daily walk and also to experience the power of resurrection in our daily walk. How can we experience Christ's death in our daily walk? By the power of resurrection. How can we experience Christ's resurrection in our daily walk? By the bountiful supply of the Spirit of Jesus Christ. The Spirit of Jesus Christ is the reality of His resurrection. By His resurrection we can experience His death. Then how can His resurrection be applied to us? His resurrection can be applied to us only by the bountiful supply of the Spirit of Jesus Christ. Now the Spirit is here. The Spirit of Jesus Christ is Christ Himself as the life-giving Spirit, who is the reality of the resurrection of Christ.

Christ's death can be experienced by us only through Christ's resurrection, and Christ's resurrection can be real to us only by the bountiful supply of the Spirit of Jesus Christ. Jesus Christ has become the life-giving Spirit, and He is within us. When we turn to our spirit, we meet Christ as the life-giving Spirit, who is the very reality of Christ's resurrection. It is by this Spirit that we experience Christ's resurrection. To experience Christ's resurrection is to contact the life-giving Spirit.

In order to apply this we have to remain in our spirit all the time to meet Christ as the Spirit, who is the reality of His resurrection. Then we have the power to remain on the cross. The application of the gates of the city is first to remain on the cross by the power of Christ's resurrection. Second, we have to apply Christ as the life-giving Spirit living in our spirit. We have to touch Him all the time. This is why the Bible tells us to pray unceasingly (1 Thes. 5:17). It is only through prayer that we can touch Christ in our spirit as the life-giving Spirit, the Spirit who is the reality of His resurrection.

When we practice the death of Christ, we will be conformed to His death, having the image of a dead person on the cross. When we touch the Spirit, we touch Christ in His resurrection, and this will conform us to the image of the glory of the firstborn Son of God. His death applied to us will conform us to the mold of His death, and His Spirit in us will conform us into the glory of His image, the image

of the firstborn Son of God. The first application of the
New Jerusalem is for us to do everything based upon the
divine nature. That is simple. But now we have an application
in two aspects: the application of Christ's death and the application of Christ's resurrection as the life-giving Spirit.

II. ITS ENTRY

Now we want to consider the pearl gates as the entry into
the New Jerusalem (Rev. 21:12b-13). This is the entry of being
crucified on the cross to be conformed to the mold of Christ's
death and the entry of His resurrection, which will conform
us by the Spirit into the image of the glory of the firstborn
Son of God.

A. Established by Christ
through His Death and Resurrection

Such an entry into the New Jerusalem to partake of the
tree of life has been established by Christ through His death
and resurrection, fulfilling the righteous requirements of
God according to the law of Israel in the Old Testament so
that the closed way to the tree of life is reopened to the seeking
believers. Genesis 3 shows that after the fall of Adam, the
way to the tree of life was closed by the righteous requirements of God according to His righteous law. Now there is an
entry of Christ's death and resurrection which satisfies the
requirements of God's righteous law.

Revelation 21:12 says that the names of the twelve tribes
of the sons of Israel are inscribed on the twelve gates. Israel
here represents the law of the Old Testament, indicating that
the law is represented at the gates of the New Jerusalem.
The law watches and observes as a gatekeeper to insure that
the entrance into the holy city meets the law's requirements.
If we have been crucified and resurrected with Christ, we
are qualified to satisfy the righteousness of the Old Testament law. Such an entry is justified by the righteous law of
God. We can fulfill the righteous requirements of God's law
by being persons who have died and resurrected with Christ
through His twofold secretion, making us a pearl before the
eyes of God, which is fully satisfactory to God according to

His righteousness of the law. To fulfill the righteousness of the law is not an easy thing. We need an entry of two kinds of secretion, two kinds of dispensing, that is, the secretion of Christ's death and the secretion of Christ's resurrection. By these two kinds of secretions, we have been made pearls, which are satisfactory before the law of God.

B. The Reopened Way to Partake of the Tree of Life Being Universally Available to the Four Directions of the Earth

This entry reopens the way for the seekers to contact Christ as the tree of life. This reopened way to partake of the tree of life by entering into the New Jerusalem is universally available to the four directions of the earth with three gates on each of the four sides of the holy city, signifying that the processed and consummated Triune God is willingly open to receive the repentant sinners into the ultimate consummation of His eternal economy. We all have to learn to speak this kind of divine language. Such an entry today is available to all the people on this earth in four directions: east, north, south, and west. This is signified by the twelve gates. Three gates are on each of the four sides. The three gates signify the processed Triune God, the Father, the Son, and the Spirit.

In Luke 15 we see the operation of the Triune God to receive the repentant sinners to enter into the New Jerusalem. In this chapter the Son is the seeking One to seek the sinners, the Spirit is the sanctifying One to sanctify them unto God, and the Father is the receiving One. Right after receiving the repentant son in Luke 15, the father gave him the best robe, which signifies the objective Christ to cover us as our God-satisfying righteousness. He also gave his returning son a ring and sandals. The ring signifies the sealing Spirit to show that the accepted believer now belongs to the Triune God in His ultimate consummation of His eternal economy. The sandals signify the power of God's salvation to separate the believer from the dirty earth. Finally, the father killed the fattened calf for his son. This calf signifies the subjective Christ for our enjoyment of Him.

This is why we have to go out with God to the four directions of the earth to be the gates, bringing God with us to present to people. This is why we have to go to Russia to the north, to Africa to the south, to Malaysia to the east, and to South America to the west. The Lord is doing this among us to spread His economy. This Triune God today is willing to receive any repentant sinner to come and enter into the New Jerusalem through such an entry which was established by Christ through His death and resurrection.

THE APPLICATION OF THE INTERPRETATION OF THE NEW JERUSALEM TO THE SEEKING BELIEVERS

ITS WALL AND ITS FOUNDATIONS

Scripture Reading: Rev. 21:12a, 14a, 18a, 19-20; 4:3a

OUTLINE

I. Its wall and its foundations are precious stones—Rev. 21:18a, 19-20:

A. We, the believers in Christ, were created by God with dust (Gen. 2:7).

B. Through our regeneration by the Spirit we became stones (John 1:42).

C. By our growth in the divine life in Christ as the living stone (1 Pet. 2:4), we are transformed into precious stones (1 Cor. 3:12a):

1. By the transformation of the Spirit—2 Cor. 3:18.

2. Through the renewing of our mind, the main part of our soul—Rom. 12:2.

3. Into the image of the glory of the firstborn Son of God—2 Cor. 3:18; Rom. 8:29.

4. All the stones of its wall and the first layer of its foundations are jasper (Rev. 21:18a, 19a), and the jasper stone signifies the appearance of God (4:3a), indicating that the entire city is in the appearance of God in His glory (21:11).

D. While the transformation work of the Spirit is going on in the divine life, we, the transformed precious stones, are being built up together to be one complete wall with its foundations.

　　E. The functions of its wall and its foundations—
　　　　21:12a, 14:
　　　　1. To separate, to sanctify, the city unto God from
　　　　　all things other than God, thus making the city
　　　　　the holy city—21:2a, 10b.
　　　　2. To protect the interest of the riches of God's
　　　　　divinity on the earth and the attainments of
　　　　　His consummation.
　II. The colors of the twelve layers of its foundations—
　　　21:19-20:
　　　A. The colors of its foundations are like the colors of
　　　　the rainbow:
　　　　1. The rainbow is God's guarantee in His unfail-
　　　　　ing faithfulness that the earth will never be
　　　　　destroyed by the flood of water (Gen. 9:8-17).
　　　　2. But the fire as a destructive element (Gen.
　　　　　19:24-25) will be used by God to punish all His
　　　　　enemies for eternity (Rev. 14:10-11; 21:8).
　　　B. This indicates that of the two destructive elements,
　　　　water and fire, used by God to destroy all His
　　　　opposers, one of them, that is, fire, will be used by
　　　　God for this purpose for eternity, and the other, that
　　　　is, water, will be prohibited from its destructive
　　　　function by the guarantee of God's unfailing faith-
　　　　fulness signified by the colors of its foundations.
　　　　Water in eternity will be used by God only as an
　　　　element of life supply (22:1-2).

Prayer: Lord, what a blessing that so many of us could be gathered by You and around You to study Your Word, so that we may see the revelation and have the way to apply what we have been seeing. Lord, be with us, even making us one spirit with You. Lord, we hate to do anything by ourselves, without You. Lord, make our speaking Yours, making our speaking Your speaking. Vindicate Your recovery by the high truths, by Your speaking, by Your Spirit being one with us as one spirit. Lord, have mercy and give us grace that we can finish this message. Thank You for the past. Amen.

In the previous message, we saw the subjective application of the Lord's death and resurrection to us in our daily experience. This is not an easy thing to grasp. In Philippians 3:10 we are charged by the apostle Paul to be conformed to the death of Christ. Paul also told us in Romans 8:13 that by the Spirit we put all the practices of our flesh to death that we may live. He spoke further in Galatians 5:24-25 concerning the application of the death of Christ. In verse 24 he said that those who are of Christ have crucified the flesh with its passions and lusts. Then verse 25 says, "If we live by the Spirit, let us also walk by the Spirit." To walk by the Spirit is to be conformed to the death of Christ by the power of the Spirit. To apply the death and resurrection of Christ to our daily walk subjectively to make us divine, to make us golden, is by the Spirit. Christ, the One who accomplished crucifixion and who has consummated the resurrection, became the life-giving Spirit in His resurrection. He Himself is the life-giving Spirit (1 Cor. 15:45b; 2 Cor. 3:17).

In the previous message concerning the pearl gates of the holy city, we used the word *secretion* with the picture of an oyster secreting its life-juice around a grain of sand to make it a pearl. Christ today is secreting His life-juice around us, and this secreting is carried out by Him as the Spirit. When we apply His death in our daily walk, no doubt, that is by the Spirit's dispensing. The Spirit dispenses the life-juice of Christ as a kind of secretion, which issues in precious pearl. Also, to apply Christ's resurrection in our daily experience, in our daily walk, is by the bountiful supply of the Spirit of

Jesus Christ. By this bountiful supply, Paul could live and magnify the resurrected One, Christ (Phil. 1:19-21).

By all these verses, we can see that to apply both the death of Christ and the resurrection of Christ, we have to touch the Spirit and be touched by the Spirit. It is only by the Spirit that we can apply Christ's death and resurrection subjectively to our daily life in our daily experience. Now we want to go on to see the wall of the city and its foundations.

I. ITS WALL AND ITS FOUNDATIONS BEING PRECIOUS STONES

Revelation 21 shows that the wall of the city and its foundations are precious stones (vv. 18a, 19-20).

A. Created by God with Dust

We, the believers in Christ, were created by God with dust (Gen. 2:7).

B. Becoming Stones through Regeneration

Through our regeneration by the Spirit we became stones (John 1:42). When Peter came to the Lord, the Lord told him he was a stone. He was no longer dust.

C. Transformed into Precious Stones

By our growth in the divine life in Christ as the living stone (1 Pet. 2:4), we are transformed into precious stones (1 Cor. 3:12a).

1. By the Transformation of the Spirit

This transformation takes place by the Spirit (2 Cor. 3:18). With Christ there is His death and resurrection. With the Spirit there is transformation. God is triune and His intention is to work Himself into us as the gold to be the base. In other words, He works Himself into us to make us divine, golden. But how can God work Himself into us? He does this by Christ's redemption and resurrection and also by the Spirit's transformation. The Father's golden nature is the base. The Son's redemption and resurrection are the steps to work the Triune God into us. Christ died on the cross with the intention of working the Father into His believers as the golden base. Then in resurrection He became the life-giving Spirit to carry out the work of transformation.

We may have the base, redemption, and resurrection, but if we do not have transformation we are still not golden. We are dusty, because we were made by God in the old creation. But God works Himself into us as the gold through Christ's redemption and resurrection by the transformation of the Spirit. This is the working of the Triune God to bring Himself into our being and transform us altogether into His image. His image, ultimately, is the gold.

2. Through the Renewing of Our Mind

Romans 12:2 says that we are to be transformed by the renewing of our mind. The mind is the main part of our soul. The second part is the emotion, and the third is the will. To transform us is to metabolically change our soul. Verse 2 and the chorus of hymn #750 (*Hymns*) say:

> God hath us regenerated
>   In our spirit with His life;
> But He must transform us further—
>   In our soul by His own life.
> Lord, transform us to Thine image
>   In emotion, mind, and will;
> Saturate us with Thy Spirit,
>   All our being wholly fill.

First, God regenerated us and now He is transforming us by the renewing of our mind, emotion, and will.

3. Into the Image of the Glory of the Firstborn Son of God

Eventually, we will be fully transformed into the image of the glory of the firstborn Son of God (2 Cor. 3:18; Rom. 8:29). This requires much explanation, but the explanation has already been released in the Life-study Messages. For this reason I would encourage all of us to obtain a set of these messages and get into them.

4. The Jasper Stone
Signifying the Appearance of God

All the stones of the holy city's wall and the first layer of its foundations are jasper (Rev. 21:18a, 19a), and the jasper stone signifies the appearance of God (4:3a), indicating that the entire city is in the appearance of God in His glory (21:11). The entire city expresses God.

D. Built Up Together to Be One Complete Wall

While the transformation work of the Spirit is going on in the divine life, we, the transformed precious stones, are being built up together to be one complete wall with its foundations. We are built up together through the work of transformation. Transformation is the proper way to build up the Body of Christ. If we do not see this, how can we build up the Body of Christ? Many speak of the Body of Christ, but where is the practicality of the Body? How can the Body of Christ be built up? It can be built up only by our being transformed into precious stones. While the transformation work is going on, we, the precious stones, are being built up together.

E. The Functions of Its Wall
and Its Foundations

Now we want to see the functions of the holy city's wall and its foundations (21:12a, 14).

1. Separation

The first function is to separate, to sanctify, the city unto God from all things other than God, thus making the city the holy city (21:2a, 10b).

2. Protection

The second function of the wall of the holy city with its foundations is to protect the interest of the riches of God's divinity on the earth and the attainments of His consummation. What are the riches of God's divinity, which need to be protected? Today God's divinity has been mocked. Some say that it is a heresy to believe that we are born of God to be His children and that we are God's family and have become God in life and in nature but not in the Godhead. To oppose this great truth is to mock the interest of the riches of God's divinity on the earth.

Those who do not see the riches of the Father's divinity do not know how to protect them. When we came to this country, we put out messages to define the divine Father and to thus protect the riches of the divinity of the Father. Isaiah 9:6 says clearly concerning Christ that as the child born He is called the mighty God and as the son given He is called the eternal Father. Some said that the Father in this verse does not refer to the Father in the Godhead, but to the Father of eternity. This twisting of Isaiah 9:6 implies that these ones believe in two divine Fathers—the Father in the Godhead and the Father of eternity. This is really heretical. Actually, the Father of eternity is the Father in the Godhead. Apart from the Father in the Godhead there is not another divine Father called "the Father of eternity." We must put out the pure truth from the Word to protect the interest of the riches of God's divinity.

Another example of the need to protect the interest of the riches of God's divinity is the opposition to the truth that Christ today is the life-giving Spirit. First Corinthians 15:45b emphatically says that the last Adam, Christ in the flesh, became a life-giving Spirit in resurrection. Some twist this verse, saying that it speaks of "*a* life-giving Spirit," not "*the* life-giving Spirit." But besides the Holy Spirit who gives life, is there another Spirit who gives life? To say that there are two Spirits giving life is to teach a great heresy. After and through His resurrection, Christ became a life-giving Spirit. Undoubtedly, the Spirit who gives life is the Holy Spirit.

The wall of the city also functions to protect the attainments of Christ's consummation. God in Christ consummated so many things. He consummated incarnation, death, and resurrection. Today some theology mocks the reality of Christ's incarnation, death, and resurrection. There is the need of the wall of the New Jerusalem to protect the attainments of His consummation. His attainments which He consummated in His ascension are for the accomplishment of God's eternal economy through His heavenly ministry. In His ascension He became the Head of the Body, the church (Col. 1:18), the Lord and Christ (Acts 2:36), and the Leader and Savior (5:31). He became our High Priest (Heb. 4:14), the Mediator of the new covenant (9:15), the surety of the better covenant (7:22), and the Minister in the heavenly Holy of Holies (8:2). Today in ascension He is also the Paraclete (Advocate) of the New Testament believers (1 John 2:1; John 15:26), and our Intercessor at the right hand of God (Rom. 8:34, 26).

II. THE COLORS OF THE TWELVE LAYERS OF ITS FOUNDATIONS

Now we want to see the application of the colors of the twelve layers of the foundation of the New Jerusalem (Rev. 21:19-20).

A. The Colors of the Rainbow

The colors of its foundations are like the colors of the rainbow. The rainbow is God's guarantee in His unfailing faithfulness that the earth will never be destroyed by the flood of water (Gen. 9:8-17). But the fire as a destructive element (Gen. 19:24-25) will be used by God to punish all His enemies for eternity (Rev. 14:10-11; 21:8). In Genesis God used two kinds of elements to destroy the human-occupied earth. First, God used water to make a flood to destroy the corrupted generation during Noah's age. Later, the people in Sodom and Gomorrah became even more evil, so God destroyed them by another element, fire. Ultimately, the lake of fire will be used for God's destruction of all His opposers.

Eventually, in the new heaven and new earth, there will be a new city with the colors of a rainbow. The rainbow is a sign of God's guarantee that He will never destroy the city. But outside of the city there will be a lake of fire, where Satan and all of God's opposers will suffer the second kind of destructive element forever. Fire as a destructive element will be used by God to punish all His enemies for eternity.

B. The Use of Fire and Water in Eternity

This indicates that of the two destructive elements, water and fire, used by God to destroy all His opposers, one of them, that is, fire, will be used by God for this purpose for eternity, and the other, that is, water, will be prohibited from its destructive function by the guarantee of God's unfailing faithfulness signified by the colors of the city's foundations. Water in eternity will be used by God only as an element of life supply (22:1-2). Water will never again be used by God as a destructive element for His judgment. Instead, in the New Jerusalem the living water will be man's divine beverage.

After this fellowship we can see that the New Jerusalem's transformed and built up wall functions in four main ways. First, it sanctifies all the things belonging to God. God would not let any of His things be mixed up with the things which are not of Him, so there is the need of separation. The New Jerusalem's wall functions to separate the New Jerusalem unto God as something holy. This is why it is called the holy city.

Second, the wall protects. In ancient times the cities had walls around them for protection. The wall of the holy city protects the interest of the riches of God's divinity and the attainments of Christ's consummation.

The third function of the wall is to express God. God's appearance is like jasper and the light of the New Jerusalem is like jasper, so the whole city will express God. God the Father is the gold as the base; God the Son is the gates to bring people in; and God the Spirit transforms people to express God. The base of gold is something within, but the wall can be seen. This wall is in the color of the stone that signifies God, that is, jasper. Revelation 21:11 reveals that the city's glory is like the glory of jasper. That is God's appearance. Today, the function of the Body of Christ which consummates in the New Jerusalem is to express Christ.

The fourth function of the wall with its foundations is to guarantee God's unfailing faithfulness for eternal security. The New Jerusalem standing upon the twelve layers of its foundations in the colors of the rainbow guarantees God's faithfulness.

Now we need to consider how to apply this fellowship. In our created state we were dust, but God wants to transform us into something which is wonderful in His eyes. By His Spirit He transforms us through the renewing of our mind, emotion, and will, the components of our soul. We are souls. Exodus 1:5 says that seventy souls of Jacob's family went down to Egypt. Acts 2:41 says, "There were added on that day about three thousand souls." The soul is the natural man, the natural man is the fallen man, and the fallen man is the man abandoned by God. If we want to change our status, we need transformation. In order to be transformed, our mind, emotion, and will must be renewed.

Once a sister told me that our church needs a hospital. I responded by telling her that this was a natural thought from her natural mind. The mind has to be renewed. We need to cut off our unrenewed thoughts. The Body of Christ is not here for a school or a hospital. After we are saved, we still have many peculiar thoughts because of our unrenewed mind. Our mind should be broken and transformed by being renewed.

In order to experience the transformation of God by the Spirit, we have to apply all the Bible teachings to our mind. We have to let our mind be renewed so that it can eventually be occupied by the Spirit. Ephesians 4:23 says that we need to be renewed in the spirit of our mind. Through the spirit spreading into our mind, we are renewed for our transformation.

Also, our mind should continually be set upon the Spirit (Rom. 8:6), and the Spirit today is Jesus Christ. Our mind should be set on Him. Then our mind will be life and peace. If our mind remains in its oldness, always set upon the flesh, that is death. Our natural person, composed of the mind, emotion, and will, needs to be renewed. Day by day, we should live a life not according to our natural concept, but according to our renewed mind. Our mind is renewed by the word of God. Only the word of God can renew our mind.

Transformation is a lifelong matter. It cannot be consummated within a short time. I have been under this renewing work for over sixty-three years. While I was teaching others, my mind, emotion, and will were renewed. Now I have a subdued will. In the past my will was like a wild horse without a bridle. I did whatever I liked or decided to do. But through the Bible teachings, my mind, emotion, and will have been renewed. Our stubborn will must be subdued to be a renewed will, which is so willing to submit itself to the will of God.

To daily submit ourselves to God's will according to our renewed will is to practice a daily transformation. A wife may say to her husband, "Don't you know, I have decided this three years ago? Who are you to change my will?" But this sister should be asked, "Who are you to make such a will? Are you God? Are you the One on the throne? Are you the One who carries out His administration through the golden street?" We are not the One on the throne. We are all His subjects. We have to submit ourselves to Him. We must have a flexible and subdued will through the transformation of the Spirit. This is the fourth application of this New Jerusalem.

The fourth application is to have our entire old being renewed. Then we accept the sufferings which are assigned to us as our outer man is daily consumed. We need to be consumed more. The outer man is consumed but the inner man is renewed every day (2 Cor. 4:16). This is the application of the New Jerusalem in dealing with our old man, the outer man, our soul with our body. We need our outer man to be consumed that our inner man may be renewed day by day.

THE APPLICATION OF THE INTERPRETATION OF THE NEW JERUSALEM TO THE SEEKING BELIEVERS

MESSAGE FOUR

ITS FURNISHINGS

Scripture Reading: Rev. 22:1; 21:16, 22-24a, 25; 22:3b, 5

OUTLINE

I. Its throne—22:1:
   A. The throne of God and of the Lamb—the redeeming God:
      1. Founded on its base to be one with its base according to God's divine nature.
      2. The source and goal of its divine administration.
      3. Also the source of its divine fellowship, signified by the street with its communication, flowing with its supply.
   B. As the center of its divine glory.
II. Its temple—21:22:
   A. The temple is the Lord God the Almighty and the Lamb—the redeeming God:
      1. The Holy of Holies, as evidenced by its dimensions—21:16.
      2. For God's redeemed elect to worship and serve Him—22:3b.
      3. To be the dwelling place of God's serving elect.
   B. As the house (palace) of God the Father, who is the King of kings, and His household, His many sons, His royal family, who are the co-kings with the Father to be its reign (22:5b) and who are the priests who serve God (v. 3b); hence, they are the royal priesthood, the kingly priesthood (1 Pet. 2:9).

III. Its light—21:23-24a:
  A. Its light is God as the glory and the Lamb as the
     lamp—the redeeming and shining God:
     1. The illuminating glory of God is the light
        within Christ.
     2. The redeeming Christ is the lamp containing
        the light.
     3. The entire city of the New Jerusalem is the dif-
        fuser, diffusing the divine light over the nations
        outside the city.
  B. As the unique eternal divine light in which the
     redeemed elect live and move within the city, need-
     ing not the natural light, the sun and the moon,
     created by God, nor the artificial light made by
     man—21:23, 25; 22:5a.

Prayer: Lord, we are touching the highest and greatest matter in the whole universe. We humbly say that we are not worthy to touch it. Lord, we take You as our refuge. We take the Lamb's blood as our victory. We do not trust in what we do. We trust in Your mercy. We trust in Your blessing. We trust in Your presence, under Your anointing. We trust in Your Word, the living Word. We trust in Your Spirit, the all-inclusive Spirit. Be with us in this meeting. We thank You for the past three messages. We hand over this meeting into Your hand for Your blessing. Amen.

I hope that we all can see that the New Jerusalem is nothing else but God Himself wrought into us to be this structure. This structure is mainly of three parts: its base, its gates, and its wall with all the foundations. These are the three Persons of the Divine Trinity. The gold as the base of the city is God the Father; the pearls as the gates of the city are God the Son; and the wall of the city is God the Spirit. The Father as the base, the Son as the gates, and the Spirit as the wall are the Triune God wrought into His chosen people to have such a structure standing in the universe marvelously and uniquely. The New Jerusalem is the Triune God, the Divine Trinity, as three basic factors, wrought into and structured together with His redeemed as the conclusion of the whole Bible. I hope that many of us in the Lord's recovery would go around the globe telling people everywhere nothing else but the New Jerusalem. All of Christianity needs to hear this. Thank the Lord that we have seen the New Jerusalem as the unique conclusion of the entire holy Word.

In this message we want to see the furnishings of the New Jerusalem. If a building is completed, yet it is without furnishings, it still cannot be used. The divine building is structured with three basic parts plus furnished with three furnishings. The three furnishings of the New Jerusalem are the throne, the temple, and the lamp.

I. ITS THRONE

A. The Throne of God and of the Lamb— the Redeeming God

The first furnishing is the throne of the redeeming God

(Rev. 22:1). Today there are kings and queens on many thrones, but the day will come when in the entire universe there will be a central city, and the center of that central city will be the throne of God. The Possessor of that throne will be the redeeming God, God and the Lamb. For eternity we cannot forget that He is not only our God but also our Redeemer. He has redeemed us back to Himself, and now we are centered around His throne.

1. Founded on Its Base to Be One with Its Base according to God's Divine Nature

The throne of God is founded on a golden base, which is God Himself. This throne is also one with the base. The throne and the base are one, one piece of gold (cf. 1 Kings 10:18).

2. The Source and Goal of Its Divine Administration

The throne has a source, and the throne is the source; and the throne has a goal, and the throne is the goal. It is the source flowing out and the goal coming back. This is the divine traffic, and this traffic is the administration. This traffic, this administration, is signified by a golden street, which is the base itself. If I were to ask, "Do you have a throne?" you should say, "In the past I didn't have a throne, but today I do. I am not a person without a throne in the universe. I have the throne of God and I am in His administration."

3. Also the Source of Its Divine Fellowship, Signified by the Street with Its Communication, Flowing with Its Supply

The throne is not only the source of God's administration but also the source of the divine fellowship. The street signifies not only the traffic of God's administration but also the fellowship of God's redeemed. This divine fellowship, signified by the street with its communication, flows with the divine supply. This supply is the river of the water of life and the tree of life. The river is for beverage, and the tree is for food, for life supply. One is for quenching, and the other is for nourishing.

B. As the Center of Its Divine Glory

Such a throne with its administration and its fellowship is the center of the New Jerusalem's divine glory.

II. ITS TEMPLE

A. The Temple Being the Lord God the Almighty and the Lamb—the Redeeming God

Revelation 21:22 says, "And I saw no temple in it, for the Lord God the Almighty and the Lamb are its temple." We need to consider why the temple is considered a furnishing of the holy city and not part of the structure itself. The structure itself is called the tabernacle of God (v. 3). The writer of Revelation tells us that he did not see the temple. Because he was used to the temple, he was looking for it, but he saw no temple. Instead, he saw that the temple was the redeeming God. Thus, the redeeming God is not only the basic factor for the structure of the New Jerusalem but also the very central furnishing. We human beings created by God need a temple. Our temple is the redeeming God as a part of the furnishings of the New Jerusalem.

1. Referring to the Holy of Holies

Actually, the temple here refers to the Holy of Holies. This is evidenced by the measurement of the New Jerusalem, which is the same in three dimensions—length, breadth, and height (a cube—21:16)—like the Holy of Holies in the Old Testament temple, which is the same measurement in three dimensions (1 Kings 6:20). The Holy of Holies is actually God Himself.

2. For God's Redeemed Elect to Worship and Serve Him

The temple is for God's people to worship Him, to serve Him (Rev. 22:3b).

3. To Be the Dwelling Place of God's Serving Elect

The holy city as the tabernacle of God is for God to dwell in, and the redeeming God as the temple is for the redeemed saints to dwell in. In the new heaven and new earth, the New Jerusalem will be a mutual dwelling place for God and man for eternity.

B. The House (Palace) of God the Father, the King of Kings, and His Many Sons, the Co-kings

The temple is the house (palace) of God the Father, who is the King of kings, and of His household, His many sons, His royal family, who are the co-kings with the Father, to be its reign (22:5b). These co-kings are also the priests who serve God (v. 3b); hence, they are the royal priesthood, the kingly priesthood (1 Pet. 2:9).

Because the Dweller and His children will be kings, this temple becomes a palace. Solomon built a temple for God and also a palace for himself separately. These two were divided, separated. But now in the New Jerusalem our temple and our palace are one. God's temple is our palace. All the folks of the same divine family live in that temple, where they worship God and live as kings, making that living place a palace. The Father is the Father-King, and the children are the children-kings. This is the reigning, ruling family, the royal family. Their dwelling place is the place not only for them to serve God but also for them to live as kings; it is a palace.

There has never been such a family on this earth. The Japanese have their emperors, the British have their kings, but there has never been a situation where the whole family are kings. We believers in Christ, who are washed by the blood and regenerated by the Spirit, are the children of God who will eventually become kings. Our Father-King is the unique Father, but He will have millions of successors because we will all be His co-kings. Romans 5:17 says that by the abounding grace we can reign in life as a king today. The entire Bible tells us that we, the children of God, eventually will be the children-kings in the King's house. The reign in the holy city will be not only God Himself as the Father-King, but also His children as the co-kings with their Father.

III. ITS LIGHT

A. Its Light Being God as the Glory
and the Lamb as the Lamp—
the Redeeming and Shining God

We cannot live in darkness. We can live only in the light. The New Jerusalem will have a particular kind of light—the redeeming and shining God (Rev. 21:23). The redeeming God shines as the shining God. The illuminating glory of God is the light within Christ, and the redeeming Christ is the lamp containing the light. God is always contained in Christ. Christ is the unique container of God. God's glory is the light of the city, and God is contained by Christ as the content, shining out through Christ.

Also, the entire city of the New Jerusalem is the diffuser, diffusing the divine light over the nations outside the city (v. 24a). We are the diffusers to spread the light. God has spent at least six thousand years to build up a city, and this city needs the light. Without the light, the city is in darkness. The illuminating light is God Himself in His glory contained in Christ as the lamp. This lamp is in a diffuser. Today this diffuser to spread the divine light is the Body of Christ. Eventually, the entire New Jerusalem will be the diffuser of the divine light. All the nations around the city will be under this diffusing with God as the light of glory and Christ as the containing lamp.

B. As the Unique Eternal Divine Light

The light of the holy city is the unique eternal divine light in which the redeemed elect live and move within the city, needing not the natural light, the sun and the moon, created by God, nor the artificial light made by man (Rev. 21:23, 25; 22:5a). In the whole universe there are only three kinds of light. First, there is the natural light, the sun and the moon, created by God. Then there is the artificial light made by man. Third, there is the real light, the genuine light, which is God Himself. Revelation tells us that in the New Jerusalem we do not need the natural light of the moon and the sun or the artificial light. This is because we have the first-class light, which is the source of all the light. This light is God, shining within Christ, diffused over all the nations.

THE APPLICATION OF THE FURNISHINGS

The three furnishings of the New Jerusalem are the throne as the center, the temple as the palace to hold the many kings who will be the reign in the new heaven and new earth, and the lamp with God as the shining light in which all can live and move. Now let us consider how to apply these furnishings. First, we have to apply the throne of God with its administration to our daily life. Every day you have to realize that you are a person who is under the divine throne and who is also in the divine administration. Just remember this one thing. This is to apply the throne and the administration. If you can remember that you are a person under the divine throne and in the divine administration, this will change your daily life. With this realization you cannot be loose and uncontrolled. Dear saints, every morning you have to apply this. You should remember: "I am a God-man under the throne of God and in the administration of God. I cannot be free. I am fully ruled, governed, by the Lord."

Also, you have to remember that you are a member of the royal family. You are one of many kings of the kingly family. Even when you are at a restaurant, you should remember that you are a king eating there. You are not just an American. You are a heavenly-born king. You should never sell your royal status. If you consider that you are a king, you would not act lightly, talk loosely, or behave meanly. You can even preach the gospel with this in view. You may tell someone that you are not merely an American but a king. Then you can start your preaching of the gospel by saying, "The Bible tells me that as a child of God I am a king." There are many ways to preach the gospel. We need this kind of vital preaching of the gospel.

We also have God in Christ as our light. Our natural knowledge, our natural ability in understanding and realizing things, is like the light of the sun and the moon. Furthermore, we have received many "lamps" from the teachers in high schools and universities. These are the artificial "lamps." In the church life, we do not need our understanding by our natural ability or our school-taught knowledge. Instead, we have our God shining within us through His word.

Psalm 119:130 says that the entrance of God's word gives light. Day after day we have to enter into the holy word; then we will see light. We will not be in darkness but in the light which is God Himself through His word. Therefore, we should not realize or do anything according to our natural ability or according to all of the education we have received. The more degrees we have, the more artificial light we have. Here in the church life, we do not need this. We have God as our unique light to apply to our life.

Today's Christians are divided by many kinds of natural and artificial light. We must be controlled by the unique, genuine, top, first-class light. This light is our redeeming and shining God. We must apply this light to our daily walk. Many of the saints exercise their natural ability too much, even in the church life. This is why there are murmurings and reasonings in the church life. We do not need the natural and the artificial light. For the building up of the Body of Christ, we walk and live under the divine, redeeming, and shining light through the word of God.

THE APPLICATION OF THE INTERPRETATION
OF THE NEW JERUSALEM
TO THE SEEKING BELIEVERS

ITS SUPPLY

Scripture Reading: Rev. 22:1-2

OUTLINE

I. Its supply is the processed and consummated Triune God—22:1-2:
   A. Signified by the river of water of life (the Spirit) and the throne of God (the Father) and of the Lamb (the Son).
   B. Proceeding out of the throne of God—the administration of the divine authority.
   C. Based on the nature of God, signified by gold as the base of God's throne.
   D. In the middle of its street—in its fellowship (signified by the street) from the throne to the twelve gates.
   E. Its main element for the life supply to nourish the entire city is the tree of life (signifying Christ).
   F. In the Spirit, signified by the river of water of life as the beverage supply to quench the thirst of the holy city.
II. The nourishment and the beverage of its supply are for the seeking believers' growth in the divine life for their building up to be the organic constitution of the processed Triune God mingled with His regenerated, transformed, and glorified tripartite elect.

Prayer: Lord, we praise You for Your victory in the past messages. We believe You will shame the enemy. You will win the war. You will gain the victory again. Strengthen us. Be our boldness. Amen.

In the New Jerusalem the number three is very striking. As we have seen, the main structure of the city is of three factors: gold as the base, pearls as the gates, and precious stones as the wall. There are also three furnishings in the holy city. The throne refers to God the Father. The temple refers to Christ. In the New Testament, Christ is called the temple of God (Rev. 21:22; John 2:19-21). We serving ones are all dwelling in Christ as God's temple. We dwell here as the many sons with the firstborn Son. The Father is the King, and all the sons are the co-kings. The temple is the palace. Also, God the Son is the lamp with the Father in Him as the shining light. This lamp is not an electrical lamp but an oil lamp. The oil signifies the Spirit, so the hidden One of the Trinity here is the Spirit. God is the shining light, Christ is the container of God as the lamp, and within the lamp is the oil, the Spirit.

The three factors of the structure and the three furnishings of the city signify the Triune God. Now we come to the third group of three signifying the Triune God. This group is concerning the supply of the city. The street as the base signifies the Father, the river flowing with the water of life signifies the Spirit, and the tree of life signifies the Son, Christ. Thus, the basic structure of the holy city is the Divine Trinity, its furnishings are the Divine Trinity, and its supply is the Divine Trinity.

In every chapter of the book of Ephesians we can see the three of the Divine Trinity. For instance, in chapter one there are the Father's blessing, Christ's blessing, and the Spirit's blessing (vv. 3-14). Then in chapter four there are the Spirit, the Lord, and the Father as the intrinsic essence of the Body (vv. 4-6). The three of the Divine Trinity are the very intrinsic essence for the constitution of the Body of Christ. The entire divine revelation in the holy Word shows how God in His Divine Trinity dispenses Himself into His chosen people. In this last and greatest sign in the Scriptures, the sign of the

New Jerusalem, its structure, furnishings, and supply are the Triune God.

I. ITS SUPPLY BEING THE PROCESSED
AND CONSUMMATED TRIUNE GOD

The supply of the holy city is the processed and consummated Triune God (Rev. 22:1-2). Our God is not a "raw" God. Some teach a God who is raw, "uncooked," that is, not processed and not consummated. But the very God we preach and teach is the One who, according to the divine revelation, has been processed and consummated. It is the processed and consummated God who can be our supply.

The Triune God passed through incarnation, human living, and an all-inclusive and all-problems-solving death. Then He entered into an all-surpassing resurrection for the dispensing of life and an all-transcending ascension to execute through His heavenly ministry what He accomplished in His earthly ministry. Even God the Father has been processed. In whatever the Son passed through, the Father was with Him. The Son told us He was never alone but that the Father who sent Him was always with Him (John 8:29; 16:32). This is the revelation concerning the Triune God given by the Lord to the recovery. No other Christians teach and preach the processed and consummated Triune God. It was only within the last forty years that we began to use the terms *processed* and *consummated* to describe the Triune God.

If Christ had not been processed, how could He have become a man to die on the cross to take away all our sins? If Christ had not been processed through resurrection, how could He have become the life-giving Spirit? Through the process of incarnation God became a man, Jesus. Jesus was a genuine man, but through His death and in His resurrection, another two steps of His process, He became the life-giving Spirit. If God had not become a man to take away sin, how could He be our Redeemer? If He had not become the life-giving Spirit, how could He have entered into us to be our life and our life supply? The supply of the city is the processed and consummated Triune God.

A. Signified by the River of Water of Life (the Spirit) and the Throne of God (the Father) and of the Lamb (the Son)

The Third of the Divine Trinity is signified by a river. The Father is in the Son, and the Son is realized as the Spirit, so the Spirit is the flow. The Triune God has been consummated into one life-giving Spirit, and this Spirit is the flow signified by the river of water of life. The supply of the city is the Father as the source, the Spirit as the flow, and Christ as the content, typified by the tree of life.

B. Proceeding Out of the Throne of God— the Administration of the Divine Authority

This river proceeds out of the throne of God. This source is the divine administration and the divine authority.

C. Based on the Nature of God, Signified by Gold as the Base of God's Throne

We have seen that everything we are and do in our move and work for God needs to be based upon the golden nature of God. Even the flow of the Divine Trinity is based on the golden nature. The river is flowing in the street, and the street is the base.

D. In the Middle of Its Street— in Its Fellowship (Signified by the Street) from the Throne to the Twelve Gates

The river of water of life flows in the middle of the street, and the street signifies the fellowship. The one tree of life growing on the two sides of the river signifies that the tree of life is a vine that spreads and proceeds along the flow of the water of life for God's people to receive and enjoy. The tree of life is not a pine tree shooting up into the sky but a vine tree creeping on the earth. This vine, the tree of life, grows within the middle of the street and along it. Thus, in the middle of the fellowship is the tree of life.

The street begins from the mountaintop, God, to reach all the twelve gates of the city. In the middle of this street is the river of water of life to flow out the riches of God to be our supply. This street with the river is a two-way traffic, coming and going, proceeding down and spiraling up. This coming and going is the fellowship. All who enter into the city through the pearl gates participate in the same fellowship. This fellowship begins from God as the source to reach all the twelve gates. That means it reaches all the ones who have entered into the city to bring them back to God.

E. Its Main Element for the Life Supply to Nourish the Entire City Being the Tree of Life (Signifying Christ)

Its main element for the life supply to nourish the entire city is the tree of life, signifying Christ. At the beginning of the Bible in the second chapter of Genesis, the tree of life is seen as the center. Because of man's fall the way to touch that tree was closed by God's glory, holiness, and righteousness. Later, Christ's death on the cross fulfilled all the requirements of God's glory, holiness, and righteousness to reopen the closed way to the tree of life. Christ is our way to enter into the city, so He is signified by the pearl gates, which include the reality of His death and His resurrection.

F. In the Spirit, Signified by the River of Water of Life as the Beverage Supply to Quench the Thirst of the Holy City

Human beings need food as the supply to nourish them, but without water they cannot survive. We need water as our beverage to match the food that we eat. All these things are signified in this great sign.

II. THE NOURISHMENT AND THE BEVERAGE OF ITS SUPPLY BEING FOR THE SEEKING BELIEVERS' GROWTH IN THE DIVINE LIFE FOR THEIR BUILDING UP TO BE THE ORGANIC CONSTITUTION OF THE PROCESSED TRIUNE GOD MINGLED WITH HIS REGENERATED, TRANSFORMED, AND GLORIFIED TRIPARTITE ELECT

The tree of life is for our nourishment, and the river of water of life is for our beverage. The supply Christ affords is for our nourishment and the water the Spirit brings to us is for our supply to satisfy us and quench our thirst. But to nourish and to satisfy are not the final goal. Christ nourishes us and the Spirit quenches our thirst for our growth in the divine life, and the growth of the divine life is for the building up of the city as the organic constitution of the processed Triune God mingled with His regenerated, transformed, and glorified tripartite elect.

Christ's nourishment and the Spirit's beverage are for us to grow, and the growth by these two supplies is for the building up of the New Jerusalem. Even today the New Jerusalem is still under construction. If we look at today's outward situation, we can see the lack of the building up of the Body of Christ which consummates the New Jerusalem. This is why the Lord has charged me to release the high peaks of His divine revelation. First, we need to release the truth that God became a man so that man may become God in life and in nature but not in the Godhead. Then we need to release the truth concerning the New Jerusalem. My burden is to release these two great truths.

Since the Lord has released these high peaks of His truths, we have to learn the new language to speak them. Paul and the co-workers around him were different because of what they ministered. Today in the recovery all the co-workers must be different. They must learn to speak these high truths concerning God's economy—that God became a man that man may become God, with the New Jerusalem as the ultimate consummation. This is a great miracle and a deep mystery.

The New Jerusalem is constructed with the Triune God as the main factors. It is furnished with the Triune God as the throne, as the temple (the palace), and as the lamp. Also, New Jerusalem is a city supplied by the Triune God—the Father as the source and the base, the Spirit as the flow, the river, and the Son as the main supply to nourish the entire city. Through this nourishment and divine beverage we members of the new city grow in the divine life and are built together.

From now on we must consider that our work is a building work by the growth of the saints in the divine life. The divine life is the Divine Trinity, who is the structure, the furnishings, and the supply of the holy city. As we grow in the divine life and minister the Triune God to others for their growth in the divine life, we are building up the Body of Christ, which will consummate the New Jerusalem. We need to experience and speak these things. The more we speak, the more we will have to speak. The more we speak, the more we will be nourished and satisfied. From now on the co-workers and the elders must know how to speak these things.

A CONCLUDING NOTE

I do expect that after the study, a study with a seeking heart and with an enlightened spirit, of these five messages, a crystallization-study of the final part of the Holy Scriptures, we all have seen clearly and evidently that the New Jerusalem is an organic constitution of the processed and consummated Triune God with His regenerated, transformed, and glorified elect. It has a threefold stress with the Divine Trinity in the three main aspects of this organic constitution:

1. The first main aspect in its structure with its base signified by the gold as the Father's nature, its gates signified by the pearls as the issue of the Son's redeeming death and life-dispensing resurrection, and its wall signified by the precious stones as the consummation of the Spirit's transforming work.

2. The second main aspect in its furnishings with the reigning center of the Father signified by the throne, the abiding place of the Son signified by the temple, and the enlightening and shining light of the Spirit signified by the oil in the lamp.

3. The third main aspect in its supply being the flow of the Divine Trinity; its base and source for the flow is the Father signified by the street, its flow is the Spirit signified by the river of the water of life, and the element of its flow is the Son signified by the tree of life.

The entire constitution of the New Jerusalem is the processed and consummated Triune God built with His regenerated, transformed, and glorified elect in His Divine Trinity in a threefold way. It is impossible for such a constitution to be anything physical; it has to be the Divine Trinity in His threefold blending with His redeemed elect. May we receive the eternal mercy and the sufficient grace of the unlimited Christ that we could live a life as a foretaste of such an organic constitution in this age for its full taste in eternity.

ABOUT THE AUTHOR

Witness Lee was born in 1905 in northern China and raised in a Christian family. At age 19 he was fully captured for Christ and immediately consecrated himself to preach the gospel for the rest of his life. Early in his service, he met Watchman Nee, a renowned preacher, teacher, and writer. Witness Lee labored together with Watchman Nee under his direction. In 1934 Watchman Nee entrusted Witness Lee with the responsibility for his publication operation, called the Shanghai Gospel Bookroom.

Prior to the Communist takeover in 1949, Witness Lee was sent by Watchman Nee and his other co-workers to Taiwan to ensure that the things delivered to them by the Lord would not be lost. Watchman Nee instructed Witness Lee to continue the former's publishing operation abroad as the Taiwan Gospel Bookroom, which has been publicly recognized as the publisher of Watchman Nee's works outside China. Witness Lee's work in Taiwan manifested the Lord's abundant blessing. From a mere 350 believers, newly fled from the mainland, the churches in Taiwan grew to 20,000 in five years.

In 1962 Witness Lee felt led of the Lord to come to the United States, and he began to minister in Los Angeles. During his 35 years of service in the U.S., he ministered in weekly meetings and weekend conferences, delivering several thousand spoken messages. Much of his speaking has since been published as over 400 titles. Many of these have been translated into over fourteen languages. He gave his last public conference in February 1997 at the age of 91.

He leaves behind a prolific presentation of the truth in the Bible. His major work, *Life-study of the Bible,* comprises over 25,000 pages of commentary on every book of the Bible from the perspective of the believers' enjoyment and experience of God's divine life in Christ through the Holy Spirit. Witness Lee was the chief editor of a new translation of the New Testament into Chinese called the Recovery Version and directed the translation of the same into English. The Recovery Version also appears in a number of other languages. He provided an extensive body of footnotes, outlines, and spiritual cross references. A radio broadcast of his messages can be heard on Christian radio stations in the United States. In 1965 Witness Lee founded Living Stream Ministry, a non-profit corporation, located in Anaheim, California, which officially presents his and Watchman Nee's ministry.

Witness Lee's ministry emphasizes the experience of Christ as life and the practical oneness of the believers as the Body of Christ. Stressing the importance of attending to both these matters, he led the churches under his care to grow in Christian life and function. He was unbending in his conviction that God's goal is not narrow sectarianism but the Body of Christ. In time, believers began to meet simply as the church in their localities in response to this conviction. In recent years a number of new churches have been raised up in Russia and in many European countries.